New Mags City Guide
Milan

For years, I've traveled the world as a design and lifestyle expert. Every time I discover an inspiring place, I make a note of it. Over time, this list has grown to include many outstanding destinations. People often ask me for travel recommendations. Obviously, most people don't have the time to find the best spots, because it requires time, and time is a scarce resource for many. That's why we created this series of city guides. Not just any collection of guides, but the best, most beautiful, and most practical, presented as a real book. I believe the ideal city guide is tangible, something you can bring along on your journey, especially handy when your smartphone runs out of battery.

Special thanks to Jesper Svangård from New Mags for his enthusiasm and publishing expertise, and to Mario Depicolzuane, our art director, whose studio's design brought this guide to life. I'm also deeply grateful to all the incredible locations featured and to everyone who helped bring this project to life.

We hope that you, as a reader, will embrace our city guide and find it valuable on your travels. After all, that's the true purpose of this book.

4728
CAPITAL GROUP

M
Infopoint
Area B

Many visit Milan without really getting to know the city. They might come a couple of times a year for Salone del Mobile or Fashion Week, but hurry on, and in doing so underestimate one of Italy's most fascinating cities. Skipping Milan is a classic beginner's mistake. Ask those who truly know Italy, and they'll say the opposite: whatever you do, don't skip Milan.

Historically, Milan stood in the shadow of Florence, Rome, and Venice, but that gave the city freedom. While others relied on tourism, Milan went its own way and became a centre for fashion, design, and finance. It is a city that

doesn't live off visitors, but from its own creative engine room.

And the reward reveals itself when you take your time. Hidden gardens and beautiful courtyards. World-class museums and galleries. An architecture where hypermodern buildings stand shoulder to shoulder with historic masterpieces. And a food scene far more interesting than its reputation suggests.

Milan is an exception in Italy. A city balancing the modern and the timeless. Like its own masterpieces, it has stories to tell and beauty to share. You just need to know where to look.

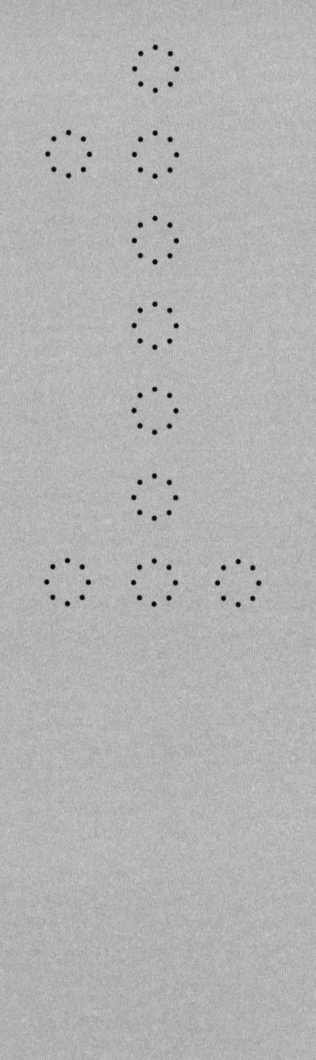

3Rooms Boutique Hotel
21 House Of Stories
Casa Brera
Crossing Manzoni
Hotel VIU Milan
Max Brown Hotel Missori
nhow Milano
Portrait Milano Hotel
STRAF

Stay

3Rooms Boutique Hotel

10 Corso Como
20154 Milano

@10corsocomo
10corsocomo.com
+39 02 2901 3581

If you've ever dreamt of living inside 10 Corso Como's world, this is your chance. Hidden within a quiet Milanese courtyard, the 3Rooms offers just three suites, each an intimate expression of the concept store's signature aesthetic. Think mid-century design classics, curated artworks, and that unmistakable blend of fashion, art, and lifestyle that Carla Sozzani made iconic. Every suite has its own personality, dressed with rare furniture pieces and full-service comfort, balancing warmth with a touch of Milanese eccentricity. More than a hotel, the 3Rooms feels like stepping into an editorial spread, refined, personal, and distinctly stylish. One of Milan's most exclusive addresses, it's a seamless extension of 10 Corso Como itself: discreetly luxurious, deeply creative, and utterly one of a kind.

With just three suites, 3Rooms distils the stylish world of 10 Corso Como into a private, artful retreat.

I MIRADOR

21 House of Stories

Via Ascanio Sforza, 7
20136 Milano

@21houseofstories.navigli
21houseofstories.com
+39 02 8907 9880

21 House of Stories injects a bright, social pulse into the Navigli district, blending hotel, coworking space, bistrot and rooftop bar into one fluid, community-minded hub. Digital nomads and gen-z entrepreneurs drift in naturally, mornings start with coffee and laptops in the lounge, afternoons stretch into leisurely plates at Domenica Bistrot, and by sunset the Miradores terrace fills with a young local crowd sipping cocktails beside the pool.

Rooms follow whimsical archetypes like The Creator and The Wizard, a playful nod to the brand's storytelling DNA, while interiors balance Italian design with a warm, lived-in ease.

Set along the quiet Naviglio Pavese yet just minutes from the lively Naviglio Grande, it offers the best of both worlds.

A social, design-driven hotel on the Naviglio Pavese, blending cool comfort with a neighbourhood vibe.

Casa Brera

Piazzetta M. Bossi, n.2
20121 Milan

@casabrerahotel
marriott.com
+39 02 305430

Located in the elegant Piazzetta Bossi, just steps from Teatro alla Scala and Brera's cobblestoned streets, Casa Brera redefines Milanese sophistication. Spanish star designer Patricia Urquiola designed the interiors of the Pietro Lingeri's 1950s rationalist building, blending heritage and modernity with effortless grace. Inside, walnut wood, Fior di Pesco marble, and printed glass echo the city's architectural rhythm. The Living Lounge pairs deep blue and amber tones with a striking green marble bar, a nod to legendary Milan architect Piero Portaluppi, creating the perfect setting for an aperitivo overlooking the square.

Casa Brera blends art, design, and quiet sophistication through Spanish star designer Patricia Urquiola's unmistakable lens.

ENTRYWAYS OF MILAN

Crossing Manzoni

Via Gerolamo Morone, 6
20121 Milano

@crossing_condotti
crossingmanzoni.it
+39 02 8689 1160

Perfectly located between La Scala, the Duomo and Via Montenapoleone, Crossing Manzoni is a genuinely fashion-forward boutique hotel in the heart of the Quadrilatero della Moda, a place for travellers who appreciate good style. The aesthetic hits a rare sweet spot: understated at first glance, then full of meticulously placed details that reveal themselves slowly, like a well-styled editorial spread. Inside, contemporary design mingles with historic Milanese elegance: decadent Art Nouveau curves, sculptural lighting, slate-grey tones, and statement artworks that feel more curated than decorated.

Crossing Manzoni, with its elegant guesthouse vibe and understated luxury feel, will charm anyone who prefers Milan at its most refined.

ART NOW

Hotel VIU Milan

Via Aristotile Fioravanti, 6
20154 Milano

@hotelviumilan
hotelviumilan.com
+39 02800 10910

Anchored in the evolving Porta Volta area, Hotel VIU Milan embodies the polished pulse of contemporary Milan. Its glass façade, wrapped in living greenery, nods to Stefano Boeri's Bosco Verticale, while the interiors balance rationalist rigour with warm Milanese elegance.

Designed from sustainably sourced wood, metal, and bronze glass, the building's undulating lines and floor-to-ceiling windows frame sweeping skyline views. Inside, oak parquet, Rubelli textiles, and sculptural furnishings create a mood of refined calm. Chef Giancarlo Morelli's Bulk Mixology Bar and signature restaurant bring convivial energy, while the rooftop pool, the only one of its kind in the city, crowns this design-driven urban retreat.

Hotel VIU is a symbol of Milan's urban revival, crowned by a panoramic rooftop and its heated pool.

Max Brown Hotel Missori

Via Lentasio, 3
20122 Milano

@maxbrownhotels
maxbrownhotels.com
+39 02 8126 0108

Just a few minutes' walk from the Duomo and the Guastalla Gardens, Max Brown Missori blends retro charm with the creative pulse of modern Milan. Its 64 rooms range from "tiny" to "extra-large," each layered with warm woods, vintage finds, and a touch of '70s nostalgia in shades of chestnut and orange. Downstairs, the lobby doubles as a lively art space showcasing rotating works by local creatives, a nod to the city's ever-evolving cultural scene. With an all-day bar and a relaxed, communal vibe, this is the kind of hotel where style feels spontaneous and creativity feels at home. Max Brown Missori is the first of its kind in Italy under the boutique hospitality group, Sircle Collection.

Max Brown Missori channels retro Milan with warm woods, ’70s tones, and a creative lobby that feels like a neighbourhood living room.

nhow Milano

Via Tortona, 35
20144 Milano

@nhow.milano
nhow-hotels.com
+39 02 489 8861

In a converted industrial space at the heart of Milan's creative quarter, nhow Milano fuses design, fashion, and art into one bold statement. Part gallery, part social hub, the hotel reflects the energy of Tortona, where showrooms, studios, and concept spaces define the scene. Its 246 rooms play with colour and form, featuring modular furniture, custom pieces by Matteo Thun and Artemide, and an ever-changing rotation of art installations. Expect vibrant interiors, pop-art moods, and a lobby that feels more like an opening night than a check-in desk. This is Milan's playful side, unpolished, expressive, and unapologetically alive.

Portrait Milano Hotel

Corso Venezia, 11
20121 Milano

@portraitmilano
lungarnocollection.com
+39 02 3679 95800

Hidden behind the grand Baroque gates of Corso Venezia 11, Portrait Milano transforms one of Milan's most historic sites, the former Archiepiscopal Seminary, into a contemporary haven of design, culture, and hospitality. Revived by Lungarno Collection and reimagined by Michele De Lucchi and Michele Bönan, the space bridges centuries of Milanese history with modern elegance. Its 2,800-square-metre piazza links Corso Venezia to Via Sant'Andrea, creating a new urban passage lined with boutiques, restaurants, and the tranquil Longevity SPA. Inside, 1950s Milanese style meets Tuscan craftsmanship through marble, brass, and rattan detailing. From Beefbar to 10_11 Bar & Garden, this is a place where design, gastronomy, and history coexist beautifully, quietly redefining Milanese luxury.

Picture-perfect Portrait Milano has been a magnet for the city's fashion crowd since its 2022 opening.

STRAF BAR

STRAF

Via S. Raffaele, 3
20121 Milano

@strafhotel
straf.it
+39 02 805 081

When STRAF opened in 2003, it instantly became one of Europe's coolest design hotels, a radical departure from the polished classicism Milan was known for. Designed by local star architect Vincenzo De Cotiis, it fused industrial minimalism with raw sensuality, long before "brutalist chic" became a trend. Inside, oxidised copper, black slate, and poured cement are softened by torn gauze and diffused light, creating a moody, tactile world that still feels ahead of its time. Each room is a composition of contrasts, burnished brass meeting mirrored walls, rugged textures balanced by quiet luxury. Just steps from the Duomo, the hotel remains a modernist monument to Milan's sleek, intellectual style. Downstairs, Bar STRAF keeps the creative pulse alive with street-facing aperitivi, live sets, and a mix of locals and travellers who come as much for the atmosphere as the design.

Vincenzo De Cotiis's vision gives STRAF its edge;
brutalist textures softened into quiet, urban luxury.

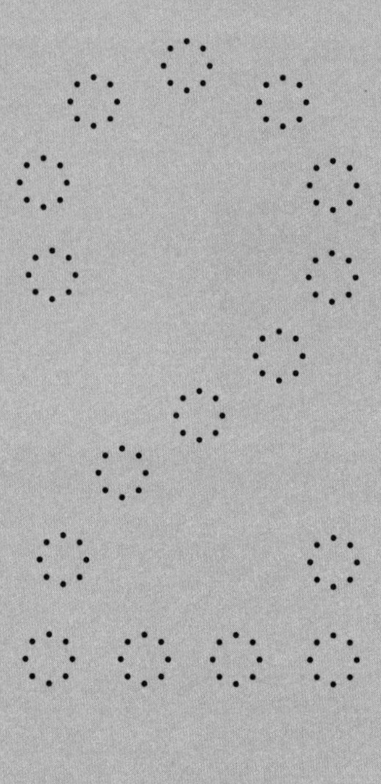

Signor Lievito
Orsonero Coffee
Fioraio Bianchi Caffè
I Panini Della Befi
Tone Bread Lab
PAN Milano
Sant Ambroeus Milano
Mercato Centrale
Ceresio7
MOGO
Bar Luce
Dry Milano
Osteria Del Binari
Rigolo
Da Giacomo
Terroir Milano
Un Posto a Milano
N'ombra De Vin
Ai Fiori Blu
Bar Basso

Taste

Signor Lievito

Via Maestri Campionesi, 26
20135 Milano

@signor_lievito
signor-lievito.com
+39 02 9167 8209

Tucked away on Via Maestri Campionesi, Signor Lievito is one of Milan's most charming micro bakeries. Founded by Latvian baker Natalija Nikitina, it's built around a 120-year-old lievito madre (sourdough starter) that gives life to her rustic loaves and delicate pastries. Expect Nordic-inspired treats like cinnamon and poppy seed buns, alongside crusty rye and wholewheat sourdoughs.

The warm, minimalist interior was designed by architect Hannes Peer, who used birch and terracotta for the walls and floor, and even found terracotta tiles for the exterior that give the room a warm, rustic feel. To make a seamless connection between the inside and outside, they painted the walls in white and used plaster that evokes Californian modernism. It's like a bit of Palm Springs in Milan.

A minimalist hideaway designed by Hannes Peer, Signor Lievito feels part Milan, part Palm Springs, anchored by Natalija Nikitina's exquisite baking.

VIA
GIOV. BATT. MORGAGNI
ORSONERO
COFFEE

Orsonero Coffee

Via Giuseppe Broggi, 15
20129 Milan

@orsonerocoffee
orsonerocoffee.it
+39 35 3478 9474

Orsonero Coffee, Milan's original specialty coffee shop since 2016, is an independent, family-run business that has been a driving force in Italy's specialty coffee scene. While honouring Italy's rich coffee heritage, Orsonero stands out by offering a curated menu of both classic espresso drinks and modern brewing methods like pour-overs.

At its café in Milan's Porta Venezia district, coffee enthusiasts can find a seasonal selection of lightly roasted specialty coffees from the in-house roasting program, in addition to guest roasters from around Europe. The minimalist design and friendly staff create a bright, calm space where both locals and tourists can enjoy an exceptional coffee experience.

A calm, minimalist haven in Porta Venezia, Orsonero blends Italian coffee culture with a new-wave precision.

1,2
2,4
FLAT WHITE
CORTADO
LATTE
MOCHA
AMERICANO
1,5
2
POUR OVER
TE

PIAZZA
MIRABELLO
1847 - 1910
FIORAIO BIANCHI CAFFE'

Fioraio Bianchi Caffè

Via Montebello, 7
20121 Milano

@fioraiobianchicaffemilano
fioraiobianchicaffe.it
+39 02 2901 4390

A Parisian corner tucked away in the heart of Brera, Fioraio Bianchi Caffè has been one of Milan's most beloved addresses for over forty years. Originally opened by florist Raimondo Bianchi, the space still carries the charm of its dual soul, part flower shop, part café, blending the scent of fresh blooms with the aroma of espresso.

With its vintage patina, soft lighting, and quiet hum of conversation, it feels like stepping into another era. Locals linger over cappuccinos and handwritten notes in the morning, long lunches spill into aperitivi, and by night it transforms into one of the city's most romantic dinner spots.

COTOLETTA - POMODORO
INSALATA
€ 6,00
PICCANTINO
VENTRICINA CALABRESE
SCAMORZA AFFUMICATA
€ 6,00
CROISSANT
FARCITO
PRAGA - FONTINA
€ 4,00
SICURO
€ 6,00

I Panini della Befi

Via Privata della Passarella, 4
20122 Milano

@ipaninidellabefi
+39 02 7602 3321

Just steps from the tourist-packed Duomo, I Panini della Befi is a true hidden gem, the kind of authentic Milanese spot you'd never expect to find here. Beloved by locals, it serves Milan's best panini packed with carefully sourced ingredients, grilled to perfection and handed over with effortless charm. The vibe is relaxed but full of energy: sunlit tables spill onto the pedestrian lane, and the staff glide through the lunch rush with easy precision. With both vegetarian options and old-school classics, plus strong coffee and a Spritz for good measure, Befi is the go-to for a fast, flavourful break in the heart of the city.

BREAD
IS
GOLD
PHAIDON

Tone Bread Lab

Via Donatello, 22
20131 Milan

@tone.milano
tonemilano.com
+39 35 1873 1109

Tucked away on Via Donatello, between Città Studi and Porta Venezia, Tone Bread Lab is a Georgian-inspired bakery-bistro that feels both local and global. Founded in 2021 by Giovanni Marabese, it's the first contemporary Italian bakery with an international outlook, a place where slow-fermented breads, Georgian khachapuri, and natural wines share the same counter.

At its centre stands the tone, the traditional clay oven that gives the bakery its name, a glowing symbol of transformation and tradition. Here, bread becomes a language: ancient techniques meet modern experimentation, from crescent-shaped shoti loaves to sustainable low-heat baking methods. With its mix of flavour, philosophy, and quiet craft, Tone is where Milan's curiosity for global food culture rises daily.

Tone Bread Lab brings Georgian soul to Milan, where a glowing clay oven turns ancient bread traditions into everyday neighbourhood magic.

BREAD LAB.

PAN Milano

Via Cicognara, 19
20129 Milano

@panmilano
panmilano.com

Since opening in 2023, PAN Bakery Kitchen & Wine has quickly become one of Milan's most talked-about new addresses. Designed by Studio Wok, the space has been celebrated in international lifestyle magazines for its refined simplicity and "durability and rarity," a minimalist bakery and bistro that subtly channels Japanese culture.

Founded by chef Yoji Tokuyoshi and Alice Yamada, PAN blends Japanese precision with Italian warmth, serving soft shokupan loaves, seasonal dishes, and natural wines in a calm, wood-lined interior. With its linen curtains, wabi-sabi textures, and sunlight filtering through noren, it's no wonder the spot has become a magnet for design-savvy locals and content creators alike. Instagram and TikTok feed on its quiet rituals, buttered toast, ceramic plates, and the soft hum of bread being sliced fresh from the oven. In April 2025, PAN expanded with Piccolo PAN, a new workshop and takeaway on Via Ausonio 23. The corner storefront serves as both bakery lab and street-facing café.

PAN brings Japanese calm to Milan, blending aminimalism in a space adored by design lovers.

piccolo PAN

Sant Ambroeus Milano

Corso Giacomo Matteotti, 7
20121 Milano

@santambroeusmilano
santambroeus.com
+39 02 7600 0540

A Milanese institution since 1936, Sant Ambroeus Milano, or SAMI, as the locals affectionately call it, embodies the refined soul of the city. Founded just steps from Teatro alla Scala by two pastry chefs, it became the meeting point for Milan's cultural elite, blending the precision of French pâtisserie with Italian warmth and flair.

Today, after decades of international acclaim in New York, SAMI has returned to its roots with renewed energy. The menu bridges Milan and Manhattan, cotoletta alla milanese and risotto con ossobuco meet the Caesar salad and lobster roll, while mornings unfold in true Italian fashion over cappuccino and a perfect cornetto. The interior preserves its classic grace with mirrored walls, marble counters, and that unmistakable Milanese light.

Whether for breakfast, aperitivo, or people-watching in the heart of the fashion district, Sant Ambroeus Milano remains a timeless rendezvous, a bridge between past and present, Italy and the world.

Milanese institution since 1936, SAMI brings its signature mix of classic elegance and cosmopolitan flair back to the city.

Mercato Centrale

Via Sammartini, 2
20125 Milan

mercatocentrale.it
+39 02 3792 8400

Located inside Milan's Central Station, Mercato Centrale is a modern food hall. Opened in 2021, it spans more than 4,500 square metres across two floors, hosting 26 artisanal food stalls, a radio studio, cooking school, and event space.

From fresh pasta and Neapolitan pizza to fine coffee, gelato, and natural wine, each bottega celebrates the art of Italian flavour. Designed for travellers and locals alike, it offers everything from quick bites to takeaway treats.

After sunset, the space transforms: music, cocktails, and convivial energy take over, echoing Milan's after-work spirit. Created by Umberto Montano in collaboration with Human Company, Mercato Centrale is a cultural hub that brings fresh new energy into the western side of the station.

Mercato Centrale brings new life to Milano Centrale, a lively food hall where artisanal stalls, great coffee, and late-night energy come together under one roof.

Ceresio7

Via Ceresio, 7
20154 Milano

@ceresio7
ceresio7.com
+39 02 3103 9221

Perched above the Dsquared² headquarters on Via Ceresio, this rooftop restaurant and bar redefined Milanese dining when it opened in 2013. A vision by the Canadian fashion duo behind Dsquared², Ceresio7 brought the city its first true rooftop lifestyle concept, a place where food, fashion, and design meet under the open sky.

With twin pools, sweeping skyline views, and interiors blending Art Deco polish with Italian warmth, it remains one of Milan's most iconic destinations. Days flow easily here, from leisurely lunches to sunset aperitivi and late-night cocktails by the pool. Come winter, the glow of fireplaces and soft lighting transforms it into an elegant hideaway.

No summer visit to Milan is complete without a drink by the poolside at Ceresio7.

LOGO MODERNISM
LOGO BEGINNINGS

MOGO

Via Bernina, 1C
20158 Milano

@mogo.hifi
mogomilano.com
+39 02 8905 1069

In the heart of Isola, MOGO is Milan's new hi-fi restaurant where food, sound, and design come together in perfect harmony. Conceived as a multi-sensory hub, it shifts easily from laid-back lunches to elegant dinners, from crafted cocktails to immersive listening sessions.

Led by chef Yoji Tokuyoshi (of Bentoteca, Katsusanderia, and PAN), the kitchen reinterprets Japanese values of authenticity and precision with Italian warmth and seasonal flair. Plates are designed for sharing, from aperitivo to late-night dining.

Designed around a 360-degree central bar and a custom DJ booth fitted with handcrafted H.A.N.D. Hi-Fi speakers, MOGO feels like a living installation. Textural concrete, rich wood, and surreal tapestries by artist Andrea Marco Corvino add depth, a visual echo of the soundscape. The name itself derives from the South African word Mmogo, meaning "together," a fitting nod to MOGO's philosophy of shared experience and high fidelity.

MOGO brings a new kind of hi-fi dining to Isola, blending chef-driven plates, crafted cocktails, and impeccable sound into a single feel-good experience.

100 LUOGHI DEL CONTEMPORANEO
ART OF BURNING MAN
Courier DREAM BUSINESSES
ROCK COVERS
TASCHEN
FUNK & SOUL COVERS
TASCHEN
LIFE
THE POLAROID BOOK
200/200 WATT STEREO POWER AMPLIFIER
Basquiat

Bar Luce

Largo Isarco, 2
20139 Milano

@fondazioneprada
fondazioneprada.org
+39 02 56814858

The Bar Luce at Fondazione Prada is Wes Anderson's love letter to old Milan. Designed by the American filmmaker in 2015, it recreates the atmosphere of a typical Milanese café, complete with pastel Formica tables, wood panelling, patterned wallpaper, and a soft cinematic glow that feels lifted straight from one of his films.

The arched ceiling echoes the Galleria Vittorio Emanuele's iconic glass dome, while the colour palette and décor evoke the charm of the 1950s and '60s. Anderson himself described it as "a place for real life, with good spots for eating, drinking, talking, reading."

Come for an early cappuccino or a quiet afternoon espresso, and linger over a slice of cake or an aperitivo. Accessible both from inside Fondazione Prada and from Via Orobia, the bar has quickly become one of Milan's most beloved contemporary landmarks.

A Wes Anderson daydream in café form, Bar Luce blends 1950s Milanese charm with cinematic whimsy and pretty pastels.

35000
ZISSOU

HO FAME

Dry Milano

Via Solferino, 33
20121 Milano

@drymilano
drymilano.it
+39 02 6379 3414

Pizza and cocktails, two simple pleasures that rarely share the same table at the same time, well not until Dry Milano came along. When it opened on Via Solferino in 2013, it changed the city's dining culture overnight, pairing artisanal pizzas with contemporary mixology in a way that felt natural and distinctly Milanese.

The interior, designed by Vudafieri–Saverino Partners, blends industrial minimalism with retro charm: brass details, exposed walls, and soft lighting that make the atmosphere both elegant and relaxed. Behind the counter, Lorenzo Sirabella and Edris Al Malat lead the creative charge, experimenting with new doughs, daring flavours, and impeccable drinks.

It's hard to mess with Italian habits, but Dry Milano convinced Milanese locals that delicious cocktails and quality pizza are a match made in heaven.

89 B

Osteria del Binari

Via Tortona, 1
20144 Milano

@osteria_del_binari
osteriadelbinari.it
+39 02 8940 9428

Opened in 1972 by Cesare Denti, Osteria del Binari turned a simple gamble into a Milanese institution. Hidden beside Porta Genova station, this ivy-draped osteria feels suspended in time, its fireplaces, wooden beams, and early 20th-century furnishings still echoing the warmth of old Milan. The menu is traditional Lombardy style: golden risotto alla milanese, crisp cotoletta, and comforting seasonal dishes that balance tradition with quiet refinement. In warmer months, the garden, one of the city's most enchanting, fills with locals sharing wine under the trees. Binari remains Milan's timeless meeting place for good food, good people, and real nostalgia.

Osteria del Binari remains a beloved local refuge for timeless flavours and slow, nostalgic dinners.

Rigolo

Via Solferino, 11
20121 Milano

@ristoranterigolo
ristoranterigolo.it
+39 02 8646 3220

Rigolo has been part of Brera's cultural heartbeat since 1958, when the Simoncini family brought a touch of Tuscan warmth to Milan's most artistic quarter. Over the decades, it became a gathering place for writers, painters, journalists and wandering creatives—many of whom left behind poems, sketches and cartoons, now framed across the four themed dining rooms devoted to photography, painting, satire and literature.

The atmosphere is nostalgic yet lively, with wood-panelled interiors that feel instantly familiar. The kitchen stays anchored in tradition: seasonal ingredients, precise cooking, and dishes that feel both comforting and carefully considered. Think classic Milanese plates, daily specials that honour the restaurant's history and Tuscan heritage, and, in the colder months, the much-loved carrello dei bolliti served on Thursdays. A timeless Milanese address where good food, good people and history intertwine.

Rigolo is Brera's beloved cultural canteen, where decades of artists and writers still linger on the walls in sketches, poems and memories.

Da Giacomo

Via Pasquale Sottocorno, 6
20129 Milano

@giacomo_milano
giacomomilano.com
+39 02 7602 3313

Few restaurants capture Milan's understated elegance quite like Da Giacomo. Founded in 1958 and redesigned by the late Renzo Mongiardino, it channels the spirit of an early 20th-century trattoria, terrazzo floors, pistachio-painted walls, embossed silk wallpaper, and crisp white linens. Its refined décor, all wood panelling, lace curtains, and antique café chairs, evokes the nostalgic splendour of stile Liberty, while Mongiardino's meticulous eye lends the space an almost cinematic quality.

What began as a single restaurant has grown into the Giacomo Milano family. Alongside the original Ristorante Da Giacomo on Via Sottocorno, there's Giacomo Bistrot and Rosticceria on Via Pasquale Sottocorno, Tabaccheria Da Giacomo just next door, and Caffè Giacomo inside the Galleria d'Italia on Piazza Scala.

An ode to old-world Milan, where Liberty-style charm meets the refined glow of Mongiardino's design.

TERROIR
TERROIR
TERROIR
STONE
ARCHIVE
BY STUDIO
DAVIDPOMPA
MILAN DESIGN WEE
17-23 APRIL

Terroir Milano

Via Macedonio Melloni, 33
20129 Milano

@terroirmilano
terroirmilano.it
+39 02 3824 6796

Terroir Milano is where Milan's design crowd goes when they want something honest, artisanal and beautifully sourced. Opened in 2017 on Via Macedonio Melloni, it grew out of founder Gabriele Ornati's long friendship with Centro Botanico's Angelo Naj Oleari and their shared obsession with biodynamics, permaculture and natural medicine. Today it's a refined bio-grocer and wine spot championing small Italian and European producers that rarely make it into mainstream retail. Vogue Italia flagged it as a must-stop for quality, small-scale food in the city centre, while Wallpaper's designers' guide name-checked it as the place to sip macerated Friulian or Slovenian wines after work.

The edit is tight: preserves, oils, vegetables, breads, ferments, and a strong natural-wine shelf, all chosen more for ethics and terroir than for labels.

A favourite of Vogue Italia and Wallpaper*, Terroir Milano champions small producers and natural wines you won't find anywhere else in the city centre.

Un Posto a Milano

Via Cuccagna 2
20135 Milan

@unpostoamilano
unpostoamilano.it
+39 02 545 7785

Located in a beautifully restored 17th-century farmhouse, Un Posto a Milano is a restaurant, bar, and guesthouse that bridges city and countryside in the heart of Milan. Inside Cascina Cuccagna, a former rural complex transformed into a hub for food, culture, and sustainability, it perfectly embodies the spirit of community and slow living.

The menu is a celebration of Italian tradition through seasonal ingredients sourced from small organic farmers and local producers, over a hundred of them, all carefully chosen for their ethical and sustainable methods. Bread, focaccia, and pizza are baked in-house using stone-ground flours, while the wine list highlights independent wine-makers.

Founded by the Milanese cultural collective Esterni in 2012, Un Posto a Milano is a rural soul in an urban setting, a place to slow down, connect, and taste Italy's agricultural roots reborn in the city.

A farmhouse restaurant in the heart of Milan, Cascina Cuccagna's Un Posto a Milano proves that community, slow living, and good food can thrive even in the city rush.

50TH ANNIVERSARY

N'Ombra de Vin

Via San Marco, 2
20121 Milano

@nombradevin
nombradevin.it
+39 02 659 9650

Situated next to San Marco Church, N'Ombra de Vin is one of Milan's most atmospheric wine bars, its vaulted brick interior once part of a 5th-century Augustinian refectory where Mozart himself was a guest. Founded in 1973 by Giacomo Cora, it became Italy's first wine shop to import French labels.

Today, under Cristiano Cora, the space has evolved into a lively gourmet bistrot and wine bar for enthusiasts of all ages, home to more than 3,000 bottles. Between jazz nights and candlelit tastings, N'Ombra de Vin remains a haven of oenological and gastronomic excellence in Milan.

ai
Fiori Blu

Ai Fiori Blu

Via Gustavo Modena, 26
20129 Milano

@aifioriblu
aifioriblu.it
+39 02 9925 3066

Set between Porta Venezia and Acquabella, near the increasingly vibrant Viale dei Mille, Ai Fiori Blu is part of the new wave redefining Milan's dining scene. Opened by three friends from the city's restaurant world, it perfectly captures the current boom of natural wine bars blending craftsmanship with fine cuisine. Named after Raymond Queneau's novel "Les Fleurs Bleues", it's a poetic space where warm interiors open onto a hidden courtyard for summer aperitivi. The menu balances Italian roots with subtle French influences, using seasonal produce from local farms, while a 120-label wine list cements its status as one of Milan's most promising destinations for natural-wine lovers and foodies.

Bar

Bar Basso

Via Plinio, 39
20020 Milano

barbasso.com
+39 02 2940 0580

Bar Basso is the godfather of Milan's cocktail scene. Opened in 1947 and made legendary by barman Mirko Stocchetto, the man behind the Negroni Sbagliato, it was one of the first places in the city to serve proper mixed drinks outside hotel bars. Think over 500 cocktails, vintage glassware, waiters in white jackets, and those famous oversized goblets of pink Sbagliato.

Its design-week legend began in the early 1980s, when the owner befriended a new wave of designers, Jasper Morrison, Marc Newson, James Irvine, who made it their nightly meeting spot during Salone. Word spread fast, and Bar Basso became the unofficial late-night headquarters of Milan Design Week. Democratic, noisy, very Milan, and still the place to be seen in April.

No Milan Design Week is complete without a night at Bar Basso, where designers celebrate, network, and quite literally take over the street.

BULLDOG
1757
White Heather
BOLS
BOLS
JIM BEAM
JIM BEAM
BOURBON

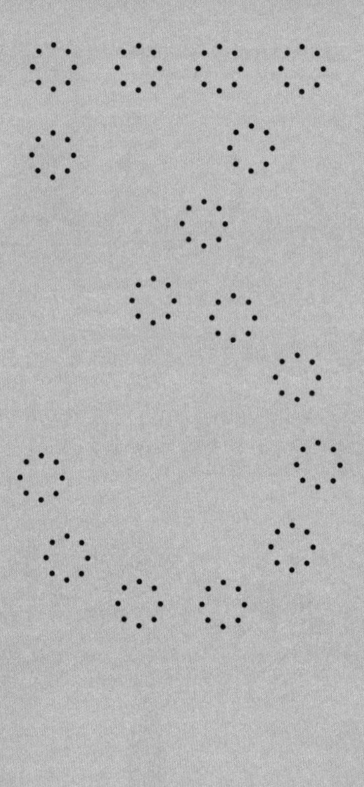

10 Corso Como
Cabana Store
Cavalli E Nastri
Frab's Magazine
The Cloister
Commerce
Don't Waste
Nilufar Depot
Pettinaroli
Stamberga

Shop

10 Corso Como

Corso Como, 10
20154 Milano

@10corsocomo
10corsocomo.com
+39 02 2900 2674

Concept Store 10 Corso Como has defined the new retail model since the 1990s. It is a multifunctional space, a meeting place, a union of culture and commerce, and marks the beginning of total shopping. A living magazine, a new model where people would live an experience rather than purchase objects, a concept store where a wide variety of facets of both culture and commerce are brought together. Today, under the guidance of Tiziana Fausti and following an architectural refresh, 10 Corso Como is developing a closer range of connections with brands, designers and partners in both the physical and digital environments, continuing to evolve a unique concept and symbol of Milanese creativity.

Reborn under Tiziana Fausti, 10 Corso Como continues to shape global retail culture with its mix of fashion, art and lifestyle.

Neighbourhoods

Brera / Porta Garibaldi
Duomo / Quadrilatero della Moda
Navigli / Tortona
Porta Venezia / Città Studi
Porta Romana
Porta Monforte
Isola
Magenta / Sant’Ambrogio

Milan

A cityscape is defined by the sum of its neighbourhoods. They are the heartbeat of a city, infusing life and diversity into its very soul. Some are artsy and vibrant, others are more serene and exclusive. Each neighbourhood has its own unique character, and we all have our favourite areas that we feel connected to. In this section, we break down the city and introduce you to the coolest neighbourhoods. All the locations in the book, along with a few bonus spots, are marked on detailed neighbourhood maps, making it easy for you to discover your favourite district.

1
7
2
9
5
4
6
11
12
8
10
3

Brera / Porta Garibaldi

1	Hotel VIU Milan (p. 33)	7	Ceresio7 (p. 81)
2	3rooms (p. 17)	8	Pettinaroli (p. 151)
3	Casa Brera (p. 25)	9	10 Corso Como (p. 127)
4	Rigolo (p. 101)	10	Cavalli E Nastri (p. 135)
5	Fioraio Bianchi Caffè (p. 61)	11	Pinocoteca di Brera (p. 177)
6	N'Ombra de Vin (p. 117)	12	Palazzo Citterio (p. 175)

Just north of the Duomo and the historic centre, Brera is the city's most charming quarter, where cobbled streets, ivy-clad façades and bohemian cafés create an atmosphere often described as the SoHo of Milan. For years, it has also been at the heart of Milan Design Week, with many of the city's most talked-about exhibitions happening here.

Start with the Pinacoteca di Brera, where Italian masters like Caravaggio, Raphael and Titian line the walls (don't miss Hayez's The Kiss), then slip out the back to the Brera Botanical Garden, a hidden enclave of green dating to 1774. The surrounding streets are filled with small galleries like Cardi, vintage boutiques such as Cavalli e Nastri, and old-school osterie where you can still order a long lunch. N'Ombra de Vin is a classic for wine lovers, while Trattoria del Ciumbia, with retro-cool interiors by Dimorestudio, serves up Milanese comfort food in a cosy setting.

From Brera, the city flows north into Porta Garibaldi, anchored by the busy railway station and the historic gate. Corso Como is the main artery, a shopping street that mixes glossy fashion with concept icons like 10 Corso Como, Milan's original temple of style. Try Solferino or Rigolo for traditional trattoria culture and afterwards climb to Ceresio 7 for cocktails by the rooftop pool, complete with skyline views.

1
2
3
4
5
6
7
8
9
10
11
12
13

Duomo / Quadrilatero Della Moda

					Don't Miss:
1	Portrait Milano Hotel (p. 43)	6	Cabana Store (p. 131)	11	Room Mate Giulia, Via Silvio Pellico, 4, 20121 Milano
2	Crossing Manzoni (p. 29)	7	The Cloister (p. 139)		
3	STRAF (p. 47)	8	Galleria Vittorio Emanuele II (p. 167)	12	Ciciarà, Piazza Santo Stefano, 8, 20122 Milano
4	Max Brown Hotel Missori (p. 37)	9	Duomo di Milano (p. 159)		
5	I Panini della Befi (p. 63)	10	Osservatorio Fondazione Prada (p. 171)	13	A Santa Lucia, Via S. Pietro All'Orto, 3, 20121 Milano

World-class culture and fashion define Milan's historic centre, where the Duomo and the Quadrilatero della Moda sit side by side. At the heart is the cathedral itself, a Gothic masterpiece that took nearly six centuries to complete, surrounded by the elegant arcades of Galleria Vittorio Emanuele II.

The Quadrilatero della Moda is Milan's fashion mecca, centred on Via Monte Napoleone. This is where Gucci, Hermès, Bottega Veneta, Céline, Chanel and Louis Vuitton compete for your attention, lined up like jewels along the street. Speaking of Prada, the Osservatorio Fondazione Prada above the Galleria is a must for photography and visual culture, offering a quieter escape from the shopping frenzy. Cabana Store on Via Borgospesso brings Milanese flair to interiors, with patterned tableware and fabrics that nod to the city's eclectic design culture.

When it comes to food, you can easily end up at one of the many touristy eateries. But the city centre has its gems too, and they are genuinely good. For a quick but excellent lunch, I Panini della Befi serves some of the best panini in town, while Ciciarà feels like a secret, a trattoria with authentic flavours right in the middle of the city chaos. If you're planning to spend the night in the historic centre, Room Mate Giulia is a cool design hotel conceptualised and decorated by Spanish architect and designer Patricia Urquiola.

1
2
3
4
5
6
7
8

Navigli / Tortona

			Don't miss:
1	nhow Milan (p. 41)	6	Aurora, Via Savona, 23, 20144 Milano
2	21 House of Stories (p. 21)	7	e/n enoteca naturale, Via Santa Croce, 19/a, 20122 Milano
3	Osteria Del Binari (p. 97)	8	I Capatosta Navigli, Alzaia Naviglio Grande, 56, 20100 Milano
4	Don't Waste (p. 145)		
5	Armani Silos (p. 157)		

Once an industrial backwater, Tortona became Milan's creative engine room in the 1990s and early 2000s. Zona Tortona was the place where the Fuorisalone exploded, turning warehouses and courtyards into the epicentre of Milan Design Week. For a decade, this was where the global design crowd gathered, and the neighbourhood's gritty charm became synonymous with creativity. But success bred overexposure. By the 2010s, the scene had shifted elsewhere, Brera, 5Vie, Isola, as Zona Tortona grew too commercial and lost some of its edge.

But even outside Milan Design Week, Zona Tortona is still worth a visit, as the neighbourhood houses Armani Silos and several great restaurants.

Navigli, just to the south, is a different kind of story. Its network of canals dates back to the 12th–16th centuries. Today, the Naviglio Grande and Naviglio Pavese form the beating heart of Milan's nightlife: fun, gritty, touristy, yet always atmospheric.

For food, you're spoilt in both districts. In Tortona, Osteria del Binari and Aurora bring old-school Milanese flavours, while Langosteria is the city's go-to for serious seafood. Around the canals, I Capatosta serves some of Milan's best pizza, Osteria Conchetta channels cosy trattoria energy, and Enoteca Naturale serves natural, biodynamic wine.

1893

0-24
GATTONEROART

3
2
5
1
4
11
8
7
6
10
9

Porta Venezia / Città Studi

			Don't Miss:
1	Orsonero Coffee (p. 57)	7	PAC Padiglione d'Arte Contemporanea, Via Palestro, 14, 20121 Milano
2	Tone Bread Lab (p. 65)	8	Osteria Alla Concorrenza, Via Melzo, 12, 20129 Milano
3	Mercato Centrale Milano (p. 77)	9	Remulass, Via Nino Bixio, 21, 20129 Milano
4	Bar Basso (p. 123)	10	Røst, Via Melzo, 3, 20129 Milano
5	Commerce (p. 143)	11	Eppol, Via Marcello Malpighi, 7, 20129 Milano
6	Frab's Magazine (p. 137)		

Porta Venezia is one of Milan's most eclectic quarters. Grand 19th-century buildings line Corso Buenos Aires, one of Europe's longest shopping streets, but step off into the side streets and you'll find an entirely different vibe. This is the beating heart of Milan's LGBTQ+ scene, buzzing with bars, clubs, restaurants and cultural events. It's also a crossroads of cultures, with North African cafés and international grocery stores giving the area a cosmopolitan edge.

Start your day early, before the queues build up, with a coffee at Orsonero Coffee, a cool micro-roastery that feels more Brooklyn than Milan. For lunch, head to Remulass, a neighbourhood favourite serving inventive seasonal dishes, or save your appetite for dinner at Osteria Alla Concorrenza to get a taste of authentic Lombard cuisine. Røst is another local gem, leaning into Nordic-inspired simplicity, while Eppol is open from early breakfast to late-night cocktails in a warm, homely setting.

Culture here runs from the unexpected to the refined. The flamboyant Palazzo Invernizzi, with its resident flamingos in the courtyard, is a true Milanese curiosity, while PAC (Padiglione d'Arte Contemporanea) keeps the contemporary art conversation alive with rotating exhibitions.

BPM
BPM
BPM
BANCO BPM
BANCO BPM

2
5
6
1
4
3

Porta Romana

Don't miss:

1	Ristorante Un Posto a Milan (p. 113)	5	Trattoria Masuelli San Marco, Viale Umbria, 80, 20135 Milano
2	Signor Lievito (p. 53)	6	Pastamadre, Via Bernardino Corio, 8, 20135 Milano
3	Bar Luce (p. 89)		
4	Fondazione Prada (p. 163)		

Once a sleepy, middle-class neighbourhood, Porta Romana is now firmly back on the map. It fell out of fashion in the 1980s and '90s, but over the last few years it has been reborn as one of Milan's most desirable areas, with property prices soaring and a new creative energy settling in.

The neighbourhood still carries traces of its past. The Porta Romana gate itself, inaugurated in 1596 by King Philip III of Spain as a wedding gift to his wife Margherita d'Austria-Stiria, was once part of defensive walls shaped like a heart. And the restored Cascina Cuccagna, a 17th-century farmhouse that once stood on the city's outskirts, is now a cultural hub with a weekly farmers' market, workshops and Un Posto a Milano, a farm-to-table restaurant sourcing from its own garden.

Food is one of Porta Romana's biggest draws. Pastamadre is a local institution for no-frills Sicilian cooking. Signor Lievito brings a playful twist to pizza, and when aperitivo hour hits, Bar Luce, designed by filmmaker Wes Anderson inside Fondazione Prada, feels like stepping into one of his quirky settings. Speaking of Fondazione Prada, it's one of Milan's most important cultural landmarks, designed by Rem Koolhaas's OMA. Its vast campus of old distilleries and new pavilions bridges art, architecture and cinema.

P

P
PIACENZA
CREMONA
BERGAMO
COMO

1
2
3
4
5
6
7
8
9

Porta Monforte

1 PAN Milano (p. 69)
2 Ai Fiori Blu (p. 119)
3 Ristorante Da Giacomo (p. 105)
4 Terroir Milano (p. 109)
5 Stamberga (p. 153)
6 Villa Necchi Campiglio (p. 189)

Don't Miss:

7 Nemi Milan, Via Benvenuto Cellini, 14, 20129 Milano
8 La Risacca 6, Via Marcona, 6, 20129 Milano
9 La Belle Aurore, Via Privata Giuseppe Abamonti, 1, 20129 Milano

Porta Monforte is one of Milan's most discreetly elegant quarters. A short walk east of the Duomo, the neighbourhood feels refined, residential and leafy, a place of stately villas, quiet courtyards and a slower rhythm that reveals Milanese life away from the crowds.

Nestled between Corso Venezia, Via Mozart, Via Vivaio and Via Serbelloni lies the Quadrilatero del Silenzio, a serene enclave named for its hush. This hidden pocket is a showcase of Milan's Liberty and Art Nouveau architecture, where the city's upper middle class once commissioned ornate residences at the turn of the 20th century. Among them, Villa Necchi Campiglio, Piero Portaluppi's rationalist masterpiece, remains its crowning jewel, a cinematic villa surrounded by gardens, a pool and a tennis court, now open to the public under FAI.

Food and drink here reflect the area's understated sophistication: Da Giacomo serves timeless seafood in classic Milanese style, while Ai Fiori Blu offers contemporary dining in an intimate setting. Loste Café brings a lighter, Nordic touch with its speciality coffee and pastries, and nearby Nemi Milan celebrates seasonality with quiet creativity.

Porta Monforte's cultural pulse beats softly, in places like Stamberga, a gallery–bookshop hybrid bridging Milan and Asia through photography, design and tea.

1
2
3
4
5
6
7

Isola

			Don't Miss:
1	MOGO (p. 85)	3	Bosco Verticale, Via Gaetano de Castillia, 11, 20124 Milano
2	Nilufar Depot (p. 147)	4	Frida, Via Antonio Pollaiuolo, 3, 20159 Milano
		5	Tondo forno radicale, Via Cola Montano, 12, 20159 Milano
		6	Section80Bar, Via Carlo Farini, 44, 20159 Milano
		7	L'ile Douce Milano, Via Luigi Porro Lambertenghi, 15, 20159 Milano

Isola means "island", and for decades it really was one, cut off from the rest of Milan by railway tracks rather than water. Once a working-class enclave where artists, musicians and outsiders settled, the neighbourhood felt like the East Berlin of Milan: edgy, marginalised and stubbornly independent. Gentrification arrived in the 2000s, and today Isola is no longer a forgotten pocket on the edge but seamlessly connected to the new Milan, just steps from skyscrapers and Stefano Boeri's futuristic Bosco Verticale.

The vibe is still different though, friendly, local, slightly offbeat. Narrow streets with hidden colourful street art, brilliant boutiques, bakeries, coffee shops and neighbourhood bars where the energy feels homegrown.

Start at L'Île Douce ("Sweet Island") for French-inspired pastries, then wander over to Tondo Forno Radicale for bread with serious attitude. Drop into Nilufar Depot for a design fix, or Frida, a cult spot that's part boutique, part cocktail bar, and perfect for an aperitivo or a lazy pancake brunch. For dinner, Ratanà has become the modern Milanese institution, reinventing classics like *risotto allo zafferano* with *ossobuco*. And when night falls, head to MOGO and Section80Bar for drinks, cocktails and snacks.

1
5
6
2
3
4

Magenta / Sant'Ambrogio

1 Triennale Milano (p. 185)
2 Leonardo da Vinci Museum of Science and Technology (p. 169)

Don't Miss:
3 Piccolo Pan, Via Ausonio, 23, 20100 Milano MI, Italien
4 Hotel Vico Milano, Via Aristotile Fioravanti, 6, 20154 Milano
5 Al Bazar, Via Antonio Scarpa, 9, 20145 Milano
6 Rossana Orlandi Gallery, Via Matteo Bandello, 14, 20123 Milano

Magenta, Sant'Ambrogio and Sant'Agostino are intertwined areas of Milan, known for their elegance. The neighbourhoods blend patrician architecture and leafy boulevards with a quietly dynamic cultural life.

Once home to Milan's aristocracy, they still exude an effortless composure, graceful façades, shaded courtyards and the distant hum of church bells setting the rhythm of daily life.

Yet beneath the surface, creativity hums. Rossana Orlandi Gallery remains an unmissable pilgrimage for design lovers, a place where emerging talent meets collectible icons. Nearby, Triennale Milano anchors the city's cultural scene with exhibitions and events that merge design, architecture and art under one elegant roof. Just around the corner, the Leonardo da Vinci Museum of Science and Technology showcases not only Da Vinci's intricate machine models but also a remarkable collection of historical artefacts, aircraft and trains. And with the Navigli and Tortona districts just a short walk away, you can easily cover the districts in a single day, design by daylight, aperitivo by sunset. Cultured but unpretentious, the three districts capture Milan at its most refined: a neighbourhood where beauty feels lived-in and sophistication comes effortlessly.

CABANA

Cabana Store

Via Borgospesso, 8
20121 Milano

@cabanamagazine
cabanamagazine.com
+39 02 7423 5292

Opened in 2024 during Milan Design Week, the Cabana Store marks the magazine's first physical location. Situated at Via Borgospesso 8, the two-floor boutique embodies the publication's distinctive aesthetic through a curated selection of artisanal objects, vintage finds, and exclusive collaborations. Conceived by Martina Mondadori and Christoph Radl, the interiors draw inspiration from Renzo Mongiardino, featuring trompe-l'oeil wallpapers, patterned textiles, and displays of Imari plates and handcrafted pieces. Evoking the refined spirit of Casa Cabana, Mondadori's childhood home, the space reimagines Milanese elegance as a contemporary sanctuary for design and craftsmanship.

Cabana's first boutique brings the magazine's opulent, globetrotting aesthetic to life in a richly layered Milanese townhouse.

Cavalli e Nastri

Via Brera, 2
20121 Milano

@cavallienastri
cavallienastri.com
+39 02 7200 0449

A Milanese retail icon for the fashion-obsessed, Cavalli e Nastri is where vintage turns couture. Founded by Claudia Jesi, a pioneer of vintage culture in Italy, the boutique curates an extraordinary collection that spans American costume jewellery, French haute couture, and Italian tailoring.

The name, Italian for horses and ribbons, instantly evokes timeless elegance and retro charm.

With three boutiques in the heart of Milan, an online shop, a tailoring workshop and an archive welcoming collectors, photographers, stylists and designers, Cavalli e Nastri transcends the traditional boutique concept to become a true cultural hub in constant dialogue with art, music and the performing arts.

sindroms
Terrible
People
meantime
flow
BOOK FOR PAPER LOVERS
NOTEBOOK
20 (para) seconds
cineforum
Beneficial Shock!
AWE AND WONDER
Breathe
GARAGELAND
Dominoes
coming home
养生
WELLNESS
System
beauty
Numéro
Homme
Berlin
MY
FRIEND
MAGNUS

Frab's Magazine

Via Guiseppe Sirtori, 11
20129 Milano

@frabs_magazines
frabsmagazines.com
+39 32 9105 2791

Frab's was founded in 2019 by Anna Frabotta, journalist and lecturer in fashion publishing, with the aim of giving space and voice to the world of independent magazines. Since then, it has become Italy's main hub for niche publications and alternative editorial culture.

In 2024, Frab's opened its Milan store in the vibrant Porta Venezia district—a space that gathers over a thousand magazines from around the world. It's a place to browse slowly, surrounded by tactile paper, bold covers, and stories told with care. Yet Frab's is much more than a bookstore: it's a meeting point for the magazine community, hosting talks, events, and projects that celebrate independent periodical publishing. Among them, Mag to Mag, the first and only European festival entirely dedicated to magazines.

6
18
HENGELSPORT

The Cloister

Via Valpetrosa, 5
20123 Milano

@thecloister.milano
thecloister.store
+39 02 4244 1633

The Cloister is a concept store with a profound passion for vintage fashion, offering a curated selection of womenswear and menswear - from high-end luxury brands to sartorial designs, workwear, and one-off pieces from unsung fashion houses.

Daniela Cavero, founder of The Cloister, fell in love with the space in 2017, when she first opened the doors of her store. The location, with its original industrial interior, is nestled in a classical Milanese palazzo overlooking the Bramante-style courtyard of Casa dei Griffi, just a short walk from the Duomo.

The Cloister showcases vintage womenswear, menswear, and fashion accessories from both national and international designers, paired with mid-century modern furniture, home accessories, and a rotating selection of contemporary design objects, beauty products, jewellery, magazines and books.

A vintage wonderland store specialising in curated vintage fashion, fragrances, footwear and niche publications.

COMMERCE
BAR

Commerce

Via Alessandro Tadino, 30
20124 Milano

@commerce__commerce
commerce-commerce.com

Housed within the storied A+M Bookstore, Italy's first bookshop dedicated to contemporary art, Commerce is a space where books become both medium and message. Founded by Amedeo Martegani, together with Emanuele De Donno, Silvia Ponzoni, and Francesco Valtolina, the project explores the intersections of publishing, design, and critical thought. Named after Paul Valéry's avant-garde magazine, Commerce stands as an ironic counterpoint to consumer culture, reclaiming the term for intellectual exchange. Part bookshop, part exhibition space, it hosts collaborations with artists, designers, and independent publishers, fostering a community where ideas circulate as freely as printed pages.

Don't Waste

Ripa di Porta Ticinese, 117
20143 Milano

@dontwasteofficial
+39 35 1945 7386

Tucked along one of Milan's charming canals, Don't Waste provides a distinctive shopping experience. Aside from their stunning collection of vintage pieces, the shop also features a range of upcycled fashion, including reimagined classics and one-of-a-kind garments that have been given a new lease on life. Each item is presented with a focus on unique style and sustainability, making it a destination where fashion enthusiasts can find distinctive pieces that reflect a commitment to both quality and conscious consumption.

Nilufar Depot

Viale Lancetti, 34
20158 Milan

@nilufargallery
nilufar.com
+39 02 3659 0800

Founded in 1979 by Nina Yashar, Nilufar has long stood at the intersection of design, art, and curiosity. What began as a gallery on Via della Spiga has grown into one of Milan's most iconic institutions, an ever-evolving dialogue between vintage masterpieces and contemporary experimentation.

In 2015, Yashar unveiled Nilufar Depot, a vast 1,500-square-metre space on Viale Lancetti inspired by La Scala's grand theatrical architecture. More than a gallery, it functions as a living stage for design, where pioneering works by Gio Ponti and Osvaldo Borsani meet new voices redefining the discipline. A decade on, Nilufar Depot remains a temple of Milanese creativity, still pushing the boundaries of the project, welcoming new visions, and shaping an even more dynamic future.

Nina Yashar's Nilufar remains one of Milan's great design temples, forever shifting, forever surprising.

Pettinaroli

Via Brera, 4
20121 Milano

@pettinarolimilano
fpettinaroli.it
+39 02 8646 4642

Founded in 1881, Pettinaroli is one of Milan's great heritage shops, a temple to fine paper, typography, and the slow art of correspondence. Once located in the shadow of the Duomo, the family-run stationer has now settled into Via Brera, where its elegant storefront continues to attract writers, architects, and old-school aesthetes. Inside, shelves are lined with marbled notebooks, engraved letterheads, and exquisite maps, a nod to a century-long obsession with cartography and printmaking. Four generations later, Pettinaroli remains a benchmark of Milanese craftsmanship, uniting precision and poetry in every detail.

Stamberga

Via Gioacchino Rossini, 1
20122 Milano

@stamberga
stamberga.it
+39 33 5563 6433

Stamberga is not quite a shop, not quite a gallery, more like a living composition devoted to photography, art, design, stationery, books, tea, and honey. Founded in 2014 by photographer Marco Beretta, it began as a small photo gallery in Porta Venezia before relocating during the pandemic to Via Gioacchino Rossini 1, in the quiet Quadrilatero del Silenzio.

Housed in a 1920s building, the new space feels deliberately deconstructed, part atelier, part sanctuary. The concept draws from Beretta's twenty-five years of travel across Asia: his black-and-white portraits of Buddhist monks form the poetic centre, surrounded by teas from his own label Auberge Thé Bleu and refined stationery from Japan and Taiwan, various books and magazines and a curated selection of soaps, fragrances and candles.

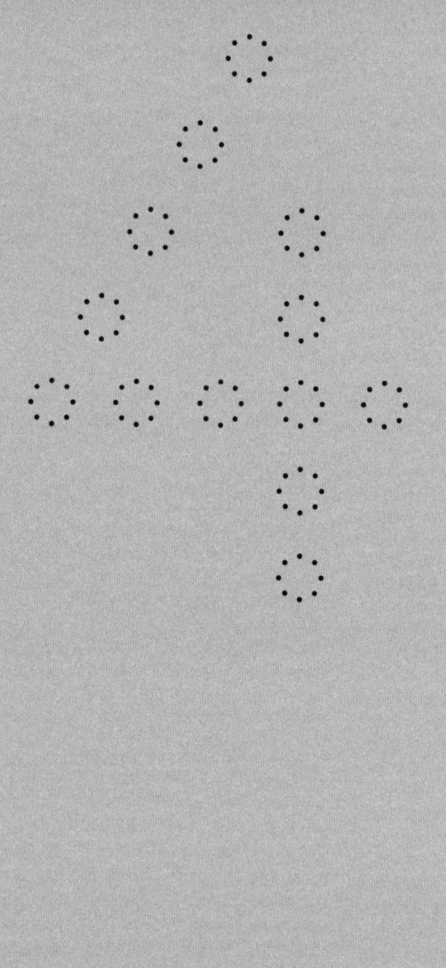

Armani Silos
Duomo di Milano
Fondazione Prada
Galleria Vittorio Emanuele Ii
Leonardo Da Vinci Museum
of Science And Technology
Osservatorio Fondazione Prada
Palazzo Citterio
Pinocoteca Di Brera
Pirelli Hangar Bicocca
Triennale Milano
Villa Necchi Campiglio

Explore

Armani Silos

Via Bergognone 40
20144 Milan

Armanisilos.com
+39 02 9163 0010

Opened in 2015 to mark Giorgio Armani's 40th anniversary, Armani/Silos stands as both archive and manifesto. A temple of minimalist design dedicated to the philosophy of timeless elegance. Housed in a former granary on Via Bergognone 40, the 1950s industrial building was redesigned by Armani himself, transforming a space once used to store grain into one that now preserves the nourishment of ideas. Spread over 4,500 square metres across four levels, the museum unfolds with architectural precision: concrete, glass, and shadow play in quiet harmony.

The permanent exhibition spans forty years of Armani's creations, more than 600 garments and 200 accessories, arranged not by season or chronology, but by theme: Daywear, Exoticism, Colour Schemes, and Light. True to Armani's rational aesthetic, the Silos reflects order and restraint, black ceilings, grey cement floors, and an open central staircase that invites reflection. Alongside the main galleries, visitors can explore a digital archive, café, and bookshop.

MARIAE NASCENTI

Duomo di Milano

Piazza del Duomo, 1
20122 Milano

@duomodimilano
duomomilano.it
+39 02 361 691

Milan Cathedral, known as Duomo di Milano, is one of the most iconic symbols of the city: a masterpiece of Gothic architecture. Its construction began in 1386 and continues to this day through the constant work of the Veneranda Fabbrica del Duomo, the historic institution responsible for the Cathedral's preservation. The Cathedral is known for its forest of spires, thousands of statues and the golden Madonnina rising above the city. Inside, the vast nave, the monumental columns and the luminous stained-glass windows reflect centuries of art, faith and extraordinary craftsmanship. Visitors can descend to the Archaeological Area, where the remains of the early Christian basilicas of Milan are preserved, or ascend to the Terraces, one of the most celebrated experiences of the visit: a close encounter with the marble architecture and an open view over the skyline of the city. The journey continues at the Duomo Museum, which brings together sculptures, tapestries, architectural models and artworks that narrate more than six centuries of the Cathedral's history and of the people who have shaped it.

Milan's top attraction: a blockbuster icon, yet still one of the most extraordinary architectural symbols in Europe.

Fondazione Prada

Largo Isarco, 2
20139 Milano

@fondazioneprada
fondazioneprada.org
+39 02 5666 2611

Founded in 1993 by Miuccia Prada and Patrizio Bertelli, Fondazione Prada has evolved into one of Europe's most visionary cultural institutions. Its Milan venue, designed by architecture firm OMA studio, led by Rem Koolhaas, opened in 2015, transformed an abandoned former gin distillery in Largo Isarco into an art venue for both temporary and permanent exhibitions. The complex's ten buildings blend industrial rawness with opulence. The gold-leaf-clad "Haunted House" stands beside the aluminum-foamed Podium, together framing a stage for contemporary art, cinema, performance, and philosophy. Fondazione Prada is a living laboratory of ideas, hosting exhibitions, film programs, and collaborations with thinkers from across the globe. Its own cinema—renamed Cinema Godard in 2023—and projects like Le Studio d'Orphée reflect its devotion to cross-disciplinary dialogue. It's a space where art meets intellect, and Milan's creative pulse finds architectural form.

Rem Koolhaas's architecture meets Miuccia Prada's intellect, a modern temple for art and experimentation.

Galleria Vittorio Emanuele II

Galleria Vittorio Emanuele II
20123 Milano

@galleriavittorioemanuele

No visit to Milan feels complete without stepping under the glass dome of the Galleria Vittorio Emanuele II. Designed by Giuseppe Mengoni and completed in 1877, this neo-Renaissance arcade is the city's original catwalk, a masterpiece of marble, iron, and light that still captures the drama of Milanese life. Locals come to stroll, shop, and sip espresso beneath its soaring vaults, while visitors crane their necks at the mosaic floors and painted façades.

Often called the world's oldest shopping mall, it's also home to one of Milan's great fashion legacies: Prada opened its first boutique here in 1913, and more than a century later, its polished windows still reflect the city's timeless sense of style.

Leonardo da Vinci Museum of Science and Technology

Via San Vittore, 21
20123 Milano

@museoscienza
museoscienza.org
+39 02 48 5551

Housed in a former 16th-century monastery, this vast museum celebrates Italy's boundless curiosity, from the genius of Leonardo da Vinci to the frontiers of space. Opened in 1953, it's one of Europe's largest science and technology museums, covering more than 50,000 square metres of history and innovation.

Here you'll find the most extensive exhibition in the world dedicated to Leonardo da Vinci, engineer and humanist, a spectacular journey among 170 historical models, works of art, ancient volumes, and immersive installations that illuminate his life and work. Beyond da Vinci, visitors can explore full-size trains, submarines, and even a Vega space launcher, all telling the story of human progress through design and discovery.

Osservatorio Fondazione Prada

Galleria Vittorio Emanuele II
20121 Milano

@fondazioneprada
fondazioneprada.org
+39 02 5666 2611

Opened in 2016, Osservatorio Fondazione Prada is an exhibition space dedicated to the study and interpretation of contemporary visual languages, with a particular focus on the intersections between technology and cultural expression. Located within Milan's Galleria Vittorio Emanuele II, it occupies the fifth and sixth floors above the central octagon, directly beneath Giuseppe Mengoni's glass and iron dome from the 19th century.

The 800-square-metre venue, meticulously restored after wartime damage, retains its original concrete structures, timber ceilings, and brick elements, complemented by new glass façades overlooking the Galleria. Conceived as a space for reflection and experimentation, Osservatorio offers a unique vantage point from which to observe the evolving dialogue between art, architecture, and the city itself.

In the heart of the Galleria, this quiet, elevated space captures Prada's most experimental side.

Palazzo Citterio

Via Brera, 14
20121 Milan

@palazzocitterio.brera
palazzocitterio.org
+39 02 7210 5141

Palazzo Citterio, an 18th-century mansion just steps from the Pinacoteca di Brera, has long been central to the dream of a "Grande Brera." Acquired by the state in 1972, it was originally envisioned as the solution to the museum's chronic lack of space, thanks to its seamless connection to Brera's botanical gardens and its ability to host collections like the historic Jesi donation.

After decades of delays, the palace finally reopened in 2024. Architect Mario Cucinella's renovation preserves the building's elegance while introducing a contemporary, inclusive layout. New exhibition halls, flexible public areas, and an open, city-facing entrance transform Palazzo Citterio into a vibrant extension of Brera, a cultural space where Milan's heritage and its future finally meet.

XXXV

Pinacoteca di Brera

Via Brera, 28
20121 Milan

@pinacotecabrera
pinacotecabrera.org
+39 02 7200 1140

One of Milan's cultural crown jewels, the Pinacoteca di Brera has shaped the city's artistic soul since 1809. Set inside a former monastery turned Jesuit college, it later became an Enlightenment powerhouse under Empress Maria Theresa, who filled the palazzo with Milan's most important creative institutions—from the Art Academy to the Braidense Library and even an observatory and botanical garden.

2024 marked the start of a new era with the opening of Palazzo Citterio, injecting modern and contemporary energy into the historic collection. With its expanded galleries and leafy new garden, "Grande Brera" is where old-world Milan meets the city's creative future, a must-see for culture lovers.

Milan's little Louvre. Pinacoteca di Brera anchors a city redefining itself beyond fashion.

Pirelli HangarBicocca

Pirelli Hangar Bicocca

Via Chiese, 2
20126 Milano

@pirelli_hangarbicocca
pirellihangarbicocca.org
+39 02 6611 1573

Just 15 minutes from Milan's city centre, in the post-industrial district of Bicocca, stands one of Europe's most extraordinary spaces for contemporary art. Once a locomotive factory, Pirelli Hangar Bicocca now unfolds across 15,000 square metres of vast hangars and raw concrete floors. Founded in 2004 by the Pirelli Group, the non-profit foundation hosts ambitious exhibitions by international artists including Marina Abramović, Carsten Höller, and Maurizio Cattelan. Its permanent installations are equally iconic: Anselm Kiefer's The Seven Heavenly Palaces, seven monumental concrete towers reaching up to 19 metres high, and Fausto Melotti's La Sequenza, a rhythmic sculpture in iron and light. Beyond the exhibition halls, visitors can linger in the welcoming public spaces, including the Kids' Room, designed for events and workshops for children and families, a Reading Room, a bookshop and a bistrot.

Home to Kiefer's towering *Seven Heavenly Palaces*, this colossal art space captures the raw power of Milan's industrial past.

Triennale Milano

Viale Emilio Alemagna, 6
20121 Milano

@triennalemilano
triennale.org
+39 02 72 4341

Triennale Milano is one of Italy's foremost cultural institutions, spanning design, architecture, visual culture and the performing arts. Since 1923, it has served as a meeting ground where art, industry and the public engage in an ongoing dialogue about culture and society. Housed in the Palazzo dell'Arte, the masterpiece by Giovanni Muzio, Triennale stages exhibitions, performances, talks and workshops that reinterpret the contemporary world from fresh perspectives. It's also home to a theatre with an international programme and the Museo del Design Italiano, where highlights from a 1,600-piece permanent collection trace the evolution of Italian creativity. Every three years, Triennale hosts its historic International Exhibition, one of the world's defining events for design and architecture.

A century of Italian design and cultural innovation lives under one roof at Triennale Milano.

Villa Necchi Campiglio

Via Mozart, 14
20122 Milano

@villanecchicampiglio
villanecchicampiglio.it
+39 02 7634 0121

The Quadrilatero del Silenzio in central Milan is one of the city's most exclusive neighbourhoods, filled with grand homes in the stile Liberty, Italy's version of Art Nouveau. At the centre is the Villa Necchi Campiglio, built between 1932 and 1935 for the prominent industrialist family after which it's named. The architect, Piero Portaluppi, was known for combining geometric Bauhaus forms with sumptuous materials, rare marbles, such as jade-green Verde Prato, were a favorite, and the latest technologies. At the two-storey Villa Necchi Campiglio, built of stone with a marble trim, he incorporated intercoms, an elevator and a heated pool as well as walnut and rosewood floors and silk-covered walls. Famously the backdrop for Luca Guadagnino's film "I Am Love" (2009), the house is also the setting for T Magazine's annual party during the Salone del Mobile design fair.

In the heart of the Quadrilatero del Silenzio, Villa Necchi Campiglio stands as Milan's most elegant time capsule, where 1930s innovation meets Art Nouveau grace.

Index

37
5
DUOMO / QU
49
44
NAVIGLI / TOR
22
40
7
36
MAGENTA / SANT'AMBROGIO

31 Cabana Store (p. 131)
32 Cavalli E Nastri (p. 135)
33 Frabs Magazine Kiosk (p. 137)
34 The Cloister (p. 139)
35 Commerce (p. 143)
36 Don't Waste (p. 145)
37 Nilufar Depot (p. 147)
38 Pettinaroli (p. 151)
39 Stamberga (p. 153)
40 Armani Silos (p. 157)
41 Duomo (p. 159)
42 Fondazione Prada (p. 163)
43 Galleria Vittorio Emanuele Ii (p. 167)
44 Leonardo Da Vinci Museum of Science And Technology (p. 169)
45 Osservatorio Fondazione Prada (p. 171)
46 Palazzo Citterio (p. 175)
47 Pinocoteca Di Brera (p. 177)
48 Pirelli Hangar Bicocca (p. 181)
49 Triennale Milano (p. 185)
50 Villa Necchi Campiglio (p. 189)

Mads Arlien-Søborg is a Copenhagen-based journalist and lifestyle expert. He holds a master's degree in modern Culture and Communication from University of Copenhagen. Mads has worked with design, fashion and lifestyles for many years. He has hosted several television shows about travel, design and architecture.

New Mags is more than a bookstore; it's a destination where art and literature converge, offering a select array of lifestyle books, magazines, and accessories. Founded in 2016 in Horsens, Jutland by Jesper Svangård and Jesper Oxholm Mikkelsen. Their dream of a space that not only stores but celebrates books culminated in the opening of their first showroom in Copenhagen in 2021.

NOTES

NOTES

NOTES

NOTES

Front cover:
© Unsplash

Destination:
© Mads Arlien-Soeborg

Neighbourhoods:
© Mads Arlien-Soeborg / VIU Milan / ElenaGalimberti / Unsplash / Pexels

Stay:
Portrait Milano Hotel: Courtesy of The Hoxton
Crossing Manzoni: Courtesy of Crossing Manzoni
Hotel VIU Milan: Courtesy of Hotel VIU Milan
nhow Milan: Courtesy of hotel nhow
STRAF: Courtesy of STRAF
Max Brown Hotel Missori: © Steve Herud
3rooms: © 10 Corso Como
Casa Brera: Courtesy of Marriott International
21 House Of Stories: © Francesca Bassano

Taste:
Ai Fiori Blu: Courtesy of Ai Fioro Blu
PAN Milano: @valentina_sommariva
Orsonero Coffee: Courtesy of Orsonero Coffee
I Panini Della Befi: © Mads Arlien-Søborg
Signor Lievito: @photolmc, Lucas Clemens
Mogo: Courtesy of Giacomo Mogo
Rigolo: Courtesy of Rigolo Ristorante a Milano dal 1958
Da Giacomo: Courtesy of Giacomo Milano
Tone Bread Lab: @about_forte / @gianfransson
Mercato Centrale Milano: © FedericaDiGiovanni
Osteria Del Binari: Courtesy of Osteria del Binari
Un Poste Milano: © POSTI srl
Sant Ambroeus Milano: © Romain Laprade / Sant Ambroeus Milano
Fioraio Bianchi Caffé: © Mads Arlien-Søborg
Dry Milano: © Silvia Sirpresi / Dry Milano
N'ombra De Vin: © Mads Arlien-Søborg
Bar Basso: © Maurizio Stocchetto / Lea Anouchinsky / Andrea Zani
Bar Luce: © Attilio Maranzano, Courtesy of Fondazione Prada
Ceresio 7 Pools & Restaurant: Courtesy of Ceresio 7
Terroir Milano: Courtesy of Terroir Milano

Shop:
Don't Waste: Courtesy of Don't Waste
Corso Como: © 10 Corso Como / Melania dalle Grave, DSL studio
Commerce: © Matteo_Pasin
Cabana Store: Courtesy of Cabana store
Pettinaroli: Courtesy of Pettinaroli
The Cloister: Courtesy of The Cloister
Cavalli E Nastri: Courtesy of Cavalli e Nastri
Nilufar Depot: © mattiaiotti / Luca Caizzi / Mattia Iotti
Stamberga: © Marco Beretta
Frabs: Courtesy of Frabs'

Explore:
Fondazione Prada: © Alessandro Saletta and Agnese Bedini, DSL Studio
Villa Necchi Campiglio: Barbara Verduci, 2021 © FAI / arenaimmagini.it, 2022 © FAI
Galleria Vittorio Emanuele Ii: © Mads Arlien-Søborg
Duomo Di Milano: © Mads Arlien-Søborg
Osservatorio Fondazione Prada: Delfino Sisto Legnani and Marco Cappelletti, Courtesy Fondazione Prada
Triennale Milano: © smarin_59 / Triennale Milano, foto Gianluca Di Ioia
Pirelli Hangar Bicocca: © Lorenzo Palmieri / Agostino Osio
Leonardo Da Vinci Museum Of Science And Technology: © ElenaGalimbert / LorenzaDaverio
Brera Botanical Garden: © Unsplash
Armani/Silos: Courtesy of Giorgio Armani / Delfino Sisto Legnani
Pinacoteca Di Brera: © Cesare Maiocchi
Pallazio Citterio: © Cesare Maiocchi

NEW MAGS CITY GUIDE
MILAN

Editor-In-Chief: Mads Arlien-Søborg
Publisher: New Mags
Sales: Jesper Svangård, New Mags

Art Direction: Studio8585
Design Director: Mario Depicolzuane
Design & Layout: Benja Pavlin, Varshini KVSS

ISBN: 97887-85374-23-3

1st Edition 2026
Printed at Print Best, Estonia, 2026

Published in 2026 by New Mags
& Helmin Publishing

New Mags city guides are available at special discounts when purchased in quantity for premiums and promotions as well as fundraising or educational use. For details, contact post@new-mags.com or the address below.

Buy the Books Online: new-mags.com

New Mags, Office & Distribution
Vejlevej 13, 8700 Horsens, Denmark
new-mags.com

NEW MAGS

Helmin Publishing
Nivå Strandpark 21, 1, 2990 Nivå, Denmark
helminpublishing.dk

This book contains a curated selection of the editor's favourite places and should be used for its intended purpose, as a guide. It is by no means comprehensive of all the amazing locations the city has to offer. Since changes may have occurred since publication, we recommend using the contact information for each location to ensure up-to-date details.

The editor and publisher wish to express their gratitude to everyone who played a role in making this book possible: the staff, friends and families, brands, and organizations. A big thank you to Fujifilm® for giving us the opportunity to create beautiful city images for the book.